Book 6 of the De...

VOLCANOES, PERSONAL HEALING AND CHANGE

Anna Eliatamby

ISBN: 978-1-80443-020-0

British Library Cataloguing in Publication Data.
A catalogue record for this book is available from the British Library.

This pocketbook also contains some concepts from the book *Healthy Leadership and Organisations: Beyond the Shadow Side* (2022) by Anna Eliatamby.

PREFACE

This pocketbook is part of a series on healthy leadership and organisations for decency. The aim is to encourage you to look at what is golden and shadow in your work as leaders and as organisations, so people can detox and heal. When we focus on the golden and address the shadow, then we are more likely to be decent in all we say and do.

Decency is 'honest, polite behaviour that follows accepted moral standards and shows respect for others' (Oxford Learners Dictionary).

We all contribute to what is golden (positive) and shadow (negative) in work and life. Mostly we operate from the golden side, but sometimes we function from the shadow side, and this holds us back as individuals and as organisations. We are all human and fallible.

Let's give ourselves permission to explore the positive and negative so that we create a better balance between the golden and shadow for ourselves and the wider world community. This way, we can contribute to a healthier world now and for the generations to come and then we may yet achieve better decency for us all.

The titles in the Decency Journey Series are:

Healthy Leadership
Healthy Organisations
Coping in a Toxic Environment
Your Own Toxic Work Behaviours
Building an Organisational Mental Health and Well-being Strategy
Volcanoes, Personal Healing and Change
Our Journey for Diversity and Inclusion in Business

CONTENTS

OUR APPROACH

This pocketbook is based on a model that we describe in our book *Healthy Leadership and Organisations: Beyond the Shadow Side*. Here are the key elements we use as a basis for this pocketbook.

Healthiness is an essential ingredient for decency. Without it, we are likely to be unsuccessful.

WHAT IS OVERALL HEALTHINESS?

The words 'healthy' and 'healthiness' refer to physical health and, sometimes, mental health and well-being. All these facets are important components for overall healthiness, but we suggest that there are others. These include synergy between purpose, values, and how we live and work; the impact of material resources and the environment, being willing to be open and listen to the incoming future, and how we live and cope with the shadow side.

All these factors, for overall healthiness, need to be coordinated with compassion and respect by our individual or organisational sense of Self. Collective responsibility for promoting the positive and addressing the negative should be present.

The golden refers to the positive parts of us (kindness, integrity) and of organisations (compassion, working with purpose). The shadow includes dishonesty, bullying, and harassment for individuals and organisations.

WHAT IS HEALTHY LEADERSHIP?

Leadership is an individual and collective function that has many intentions. This usually includes an aim to serve human beings and/or something else. Some people operationalize leadership ethically and positively to serve others. Others will have another focus, such as a profit motive, alongside wanting to be ethical.

Healthy leadership happens when the individual or the group do their utmost to serve others ethically and respectfully, while acknowledging that there can be negativity and being willing to address it and heal. They remain flexible and open to sensing the incoming future.

Being and growing as a healthy leader ensures decency in yourself and in how you act at work.

WHAT IS A HEALTHY ORGANISATION?

Why do organisations exist? To enact a greater purpose, sometimes forgotten as the organisation becomes bigger and veers from the intended path.

A healthy organisation ensures it remains true to its purpose, and to do no harm to humans or the planet. <u>Do no harm</u>. The organisation always endeavours to provide a nourishing culture and structure within which people can grow and flourish in their work to achieve that purpose. A healthy organisation works to recognise and address unhealthy elements, is amenable to change, and will consider possible futures while operating in the present.

Decency is a core essential and its use flows naturally throughout the organization. People do not have to think about the need to be decent, they just are. Thus, the organization contributes to the greater decency we need for the world.

INTRODUCTION

"We are so accustomed to disguise ourselves to others that in the end, we become disguised to ourselves."
François de la Rochefoucauld

"If our dreams get broken along the way, we have to make new ones from the pieces.'
Erin Quinn, Derry Girls (Lisa McGee)

As adults, we have built a repertoire of behaviours, words, emotions, and stories to justify how we are in the world with ourselves, others, and our physical environment. Most of the time, this works for us and so we don't stop to look at ourselves in any meaningful way. We carry on as human beings living decently, supposedly in harmony with ourselves, others, and the world. We have an extensive repertoire of positive behaviours, emotions and thoughts and, hopefully, just a few negative ones.

Some of us will have had difficulties or trauma in our past. It is extremely rare that we look at them, heal and build healthily. Often we cover these up, learn unhealthy ways of dismissing or denying them. So, they continue to fester, even if we have a myriad of wonderful positive ways to survive.

Inevitably, there will come a time when the unresolved bursts through or is triggered by something in our current life. These are the 'volcanoes' in our lives.

Anjula had always been heavier than was healthy. She would only buy mechanical bathroom scales because she could manipulate them more easily. Each new scale would be altered to weigh two pounds lighter, and she had learned to stand on them so that she 'weighed' less. She started exercising and so she ignored the scales. Anjula told herself that the reason she had to buy larger sizes was because the manufacturers had changed their criteria for sizing.

Rory (they, them) was ambitious and very focused. Nothing got in their way. A teacher had once told them they were not intelligent and that their family and background would always hold them back. They believed this until they moved in with their aunt, who helped them develop a different view. They learned to ignore their family's ways- always unscrupulous. If there was an illegal and easy way, the family would find it and use it.

Rory decided they needed to be more ambitious and creative. A 'friend' told them they could progress further if they would 'work around' some of the company's financial rules. They tried it and were successful. They decided they will carry on but with care.

Like Anjula and Rory, we can carry on ignoring our hidden volcanoes and other issues. Or we can stop and think about our past, how this affects us in the present day and then heal, dousing the volcanoes or fires.

Doing this will help us learn to be more decent with ourselves and, therefore, with others and the world. The unresolved and hidden elements can interfere with our desire and attempt to be decent.

In this guide, we have given you a series of reflections to learn about how you have been living and how you can change.

THE PAST

We have many layers for who we are. Our baseline is our past. What has happened to us has shaped us. For example, the food we prefer, the clothes we wear, the professions we choose and the relationships we have.

Our history contains both positive events and people, and for some of us, there are negatives. Positives include parents who gave you freedom and unwavering support in quiet, unobtrusive ways. Alternatively, a parent who took a dislike to us and favoured other siblings is a negative. An uncle who had an unusual sexual interest in his nieces and would take every opportunity to touch them at family gatherings. These leave a mark on us and sometimes they stray into our everyday lives. They are ever present.

Let's use the metaphor of volcanoes to explore how the past and its negatives affect us. There are many types of volcanoes, small and large ones, those that have been dormant and are very unlikely to explode and erupt, those that could become active and those that just simmer. Sometimes, they erupt by themselves suddenly or are triggered by something in ourselves or the world. The impact of a volcano can vary depending on the trigger, us and the circumstances in which we find ourselves.

Ronya's mother was extremely manipulative. It was what she knew and had become comfortable with. Ronya had learned to ignore this as she was growing up and as an adult, she also ignored or avoided others who used similar behaviours. She felt that this was a mature approach. It allowed her to function and ignore the past when it re-emerged in the present. She also did not 'see' that she had similar behaviours. Her sister, Berta, decided to look at her history. With professional help, she identified how the past was still present. This helped her to heal.

Ronya's volcanoes were mainly those that were dormant and could erupt, but which she suppressed.

Berta's volcanoes were also dormant, but she examined them and developed a series of methods of recognising ways in which they could erupt, e.g. working with someone who was very devious.

We all have a range of these volcanoes and an assortment of strategies to acknowledge, deny, or deal with them. These are the issues that can have a very negative effect, especially if we try to deny their effect in our current life. The quantity and volume of the volcanoes in our lives is not always dependent on how much trauma we have experienced. It is how important the event and reaction have been to us. Someone whose parents sometimes ignored them while providing the essentials could have as many volcanoes as someone who was serially abused.

We will use the metaphor of a calm 'breath' of fresh air to describe the positives. This 'breath' is always around us and we can, when we need, stop, recall it and refresh ourselves. For example, remembering a brave and favourite aunt when you lack courage.

Using these metaphors, let's explore the impact of the past on life. Please try one or more of the reflections described below. Perhaps keep a notebook with you to note down what you have learned.

Remember that it is important to do this when you feel safe enough and ready to do this exploration. Being open to this journey is very important. If you are not, then you may not explore in the best way possible and you may even sabotage yourself.

Please be extra cautious if you have experienced trauma or significant difficulties in your life. If you want to explore, it may be wiser to do this work with a good and trusted person or a mental health professional, such as a counsellor or clinical psychologist.

Here are some reflections to use.

Perhaps start with drawing a timeline of your history from the moment you were born. Simply describe the events that took place and the significant people you encountered. If you can, think about the wider environment, e.g. your community, world affairs that may have affected your life.

Alternatively, you could 'create' a documentary about your life. Who are the key actors? What is the timeline? What are the key scenes? Remember to include both positives and negatives.

Now, please use the reflections below. Take your time to pause and stop as you wish.

MY LIFE

This diagram outlines the key areas of our lives. Please find a quiet time and place. Have the diagram in front of you. Reflect on it for five minutes in silence. Note down any reflections, then answer the questions below.

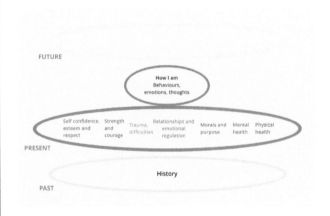

Describe all the behaviours, thoughts and emotions you experienced in the last month.

Remember to think about both the positives (helpful) and negatives (unhelpful).

What were the key events in your history? Who were the significant people? How do these influence you today? Whose 'voice' stays with you?

How much self-confidence, self-esteem, and respect do you have?

How much strength and courage do you have?

Far too much   Not enough

◄──►

What traumatic or difficult events happened to you? How do they have an impact today?

What strategies do you use to cope? You can choose more than one.

❒   Am realistic and have resolved most issues
❒   Deny what happened
❒   Dismiss and ignore what occurred
❒   Distract myself by focusing on other issues
❒   Am easily triggered back to what happened
❒   Suddenly get stuck or flummoxed when a trigger appears
❒   Have good coping strategies to cope with the influence of what happened
❒   Numbing and suppressing
❒   Self-sabotage

Relationships

Who is in your life? Who is supportive of you and who is not?

Emotional regulation

Which emotions do you allow in your life? Where, in your body, do you feel them? How good are you at managing and regulating them?

Very poor regulation   Very good regulation

Morals and purpose

What are your morals? Describe your purpose. How much do you use them in your daily life?

Very limited impact   Adhere to them rigidly

Mental health

How much does your mental health affect your daily life? How well do you look after yourself?

Physical health

How much does your physical health affect your daily life? How well do you look after your physical health?

The external world

How much does the external world influence you- where you live and work, the impact of climate change, your community, news and the media, etc.? How important are material goods to you?

Based on all your answers, how would you describe yourself? What is your identity?

I am _____

What does your statement say about your approach to decency? What would your close friends, partners and families say about your statement?

VOLCANOES AND BREATHS OF CALM

We all have unresolved issues in our past which can filter through to the present. The problem is that we don't always recognise them and so they continue to have an adverse effect on our lives- the volcanoes (orange and brown). Similarly, we don't always realise that there are wonderful breaths of calm (green) from our past that can have a positive influence in our present-day life.

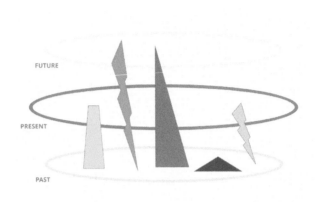

Think back to the last year. What really difficult and awkward moments did you have? How did you cope in the moment and afterwards? How were these moments triggered and by what? What was the link to your past and unresolved matters?

What types of volcanoes do you have in your life?

- ❒ Dormant and resolved
- ❒ Minor, unresolved and unlikely to erupt
- ❒ Minor and sometimes erupting
- ❒ Major and often erupting
- ❒ Major, kept at bay and unlikely to erupt
- ❒ Another type

What triggers them?

- ❏ Work
- ❏ A person
- ❏ Stress
- ❏ Sudden and unexpected event
- ❏ Anxiety
- ❏ Worry, e.g. about the climate
- ❏ Something else

Now think of brilliant moments that you had. What or who, from the past, really helped you? What are your calm breaths?

How do the volcanoes and calm breaths affect your attempt to be decent?

Make a note of your learning.

CURRENT PROBLEM(S)

Having identified your calm breaths and volcanoes, perhaps think of a specific issue that is troubling you or one you want to learn more about. Here are some questions for you.

What is it? What triggers it? How is it maintained? And the link to the volcanoes? How much do you want to change your approach?

PROTECTIVE AND RISK FACTORS

We each have a range of factors that are protective and allow us to live our lives, e.g. an interesting job. We also have risk factors, e.g. financial problems, difficult relationship with a partner. It is worth stopping and identifying the ones that apply to you.

What are your current protective factors?

What are your risk factors?

UNDERSTANDING HOW YOU CHANGE

The path of change

This diagram depicts the steps to changing from your current self to the re-shaped self. It is important to take a few moments to understand how you change- both voluntarily and otherwise. If you are ready to change, what is the path you are likely to follow? If you are reluctant to change, what do you do?

We can, sometimes, choose to change and then do so. But then we revert to old habits. This can be our pattern for change which means that we simply do not change for the better in the long term. How much is this your pattern?

Think about your current repertoire of habits (behaviours, thoughts and emotions). Which ones help you to maintain the current Self in a positive way and which ones interfere with your positivity? What is the future Self that you want? What new habits do you need? How can you say goodbye to the old Self?

Make a note of what you have learned.

Sybil had a lifelong problem with weight. It was a family issue, as was the tendency to obsess. She joined a slimming club and was very successful. It took her three months to adjust to the new regime, which she fought for a long time. Sybil ignored the new advice and simply worked out her own routine, which was successful but not sustainable. Even though she lost a lot of weight, she was always at risk of putting it back on. Until she sat down and worked out her healthy and unhealthy eating habits, changed her mindset to one of eating healthily for nutrition and found other ways of dealing with her anxiety and obsessive tendencies. She also realised that she had to change her identity to one where she did not need to go back into the cycle of gaining, then losing weight.

Dominic wanted to become more assertive at work. To do so, he needed to give himself permission to acknowledge that he preferred slow change with support and that there was a strong risk of self-sabotage. He then looked at how he could adapt his self-respect, emotions, and mindset so that he could become more confident.

EXPLAINING
YOUR FINDINGS

Now that you have a clearer sense of how you are and the influence of your past, let's explore how this affects you in the day to day.

We all have difficulties and, for some, trauma in our past. Some of this may have been resolved healthily and others not. It is how we recognise and acknowledge our past that matters. Not necessarily whether it was traumatic. It is best to accept our past and know that it may still have an influence in our daily lives. Once we do that, then we can grow and flourish.

So, the key is the extent to which we can function in real life, not how troubled is our past. How we function varies from day to day. How we operate depends on the balance we have between our golden and positives and the hidden volcanoes in our life.

Sometimes, we can cope and have a good balance for a long while and then we lose our poise, and we find life difficult. Sometimes, we can work on finding the balance again. This can be instantaneous, or we may need some time or help to recover.

Please use these scales to identify where you are on a daily and weekly basis.

Overall, what is uppermost?

Positives and calm breaths   Negatives and volcanoes

How effective are your strategies for enabling the positives and calm breaths?

Ineffective   Effective

How effective are your strategies for managing the volcanoes and the factors (internal and external) that trigger eruptions?

Ineffective   Effective

Please make some notes, summarise your responses. Now reflect on what you have written.

Leave the notes somewhere safe for about a week. Now and again, return to them and reflect again. Any changes?

Having done this, please now move to the next section.

HOW DO I HEAL AND CHANGE?

It is far easier to remain as we are, especially as adults. But if we give ourselves permission, we can, at any age, start the journey for healing and recovery. Usually, the journey is slow and progressive. It is important to stay open to exploring and learning, knowing that there will be surprises even when we say that we are exploring one set of difficulties and volcanoes.

Marta had given herself permission to explore the fact that she had had a tough childhood with overbearing parents. She was working on reconciling and making peace with her past and changing how she trusted and interacted with people. Marta wanted to become more confident. She was proud of the progress she had made in the last three months.

One day, while browsing through YouTube, she came across a recent video of a favourite singer of hers, Jackson Browne. His music had given her solace when she was younger. However, she could not watch it as it showed her how old he had become.

When she had calmed down, she realised what she had done. She noted it and said that she would think about what her reaction meant in terms of her growing older.

We are good at self-deception even if we are overall positive and decent. Let's give ourselves permission to change and be more than we are. We need to look at key parts of ourselves and we outline these below with some suggestions.

You could choose to work on all the parts recommended below. But that might be too much. Why not read what we have written and then choose a few areas where you can start, perhaps something with a little challenge?

Make sure that you are realistic and choose to change something that you can either control or influence. Your chances of success will be greater.

Rodo decided to be more confident with her partner, who was very domineering. She thought about it and decided that she could not make him change, but she could influence him by changing how she responded. She quietly became more assertive, and it worked. It gave them both time to adjust to the differences.

Whatever you choose, it is vital that you create a plan with actionable steps.

MY FUTURE SELF

If we want to change, we must redefine ourselves. Think back to how you described your identity and everything else that you have learned.

What would you like to change in terms of your identity? For example, if you have a pattern of changing and then reverting to old habits, could you say that you will become someone who changes permanently?

How would you describe your new self? What are the associated beliefs, thoughts, and actions? How will you say goodbye to your old identity and habits?

I am _____

My beliefs are _____

The thoughts and actions I would like to use are:

What steps do you need to take to say goodbye to your old self and associated habits?

How will you ensure you work on changing?

CHANGING

Think back to your reflections on how you change. Who do you need in your present life to make sure that you change healthily and positively? If you tend to change and then revert, what can you do to alter this pattern? What would be the best thing if you changed? What could frighten? Therefore, what steps should you take to ensure that you live your new identity?

Sofia had been trying to lose weight for the longest time. She joined a slimming group, and, with the great help of the consultant and the group, she lost 10 kilos. Sofia wanted to lose another 4 kilos to be within a healthy weight range. She kept stalling, putting on .5kilos, then losing it, then putting it back on again. Sofia wondered why. She explored this using a reflection.

What would be the best thing if I reached my goal? *I would feel good.*

What would be the worst and scariest thing? *Well, I might go back to how I was the last time I was that slim. Bad relationships, lacking in confidence.*

Aha, that was over ten years ago. Let me reframe. I am different and wiser in terms of my relationships. I am already dealing well with people reacting to my changed body shape. There is nothing to fear.

Alternatively, stop and look at the old and negative habits you are using to prevent change. How can you nullify them? For example, in Sofia's case, she kept wanting to eat too much in the evenings, so she had large bowls of salad available at night as a substitute.

Riger became very aggressive easily. Even though they had been sent on a variety of anger management courses. Riger had created a good action plan which sometimes worked but did not stop the feelings arising, especially with a particular colleague. Whenever the feelings arose, Riger looked at a postcard on their phone which said, "ANGER." They touched the screen, took a deep breath, moved onto the next screen, which said, "LET GO AND BREATHE.' That helped.

Think about the steps you need to change and adopt your new identity? What will help? Who could support you? How could you self-sabotage? If that happens, what should you do? How will you reward yourself once you change?

Please note down your learning.

BOUNDARIES

We rarely think about the rules and boundaries of our lives. They reinforce our identity, both positively and negatively. Take a moment to stop and think about your boundaries in these key areas and see if they need to change.

Emotions - how do you allow them in your life? What is helpful? What is not, e.g. suppression?

Relationships - what rules do you have for those closest to you? And for acquaintances?

Physical - who can touch you or not?

Financial - how good are you at managing your finances?

Time, strength, and energy - how good are you with using your time, strength, and energy?

Cognitive capacities (memory, thinking, decision making, attention) - how efficiently do you use these skills?

Problem solving - how effective are your current methods for problem solving? What needs to change?

Self-care - how well do you look after yourself, ensuring that the positives are uppermost, and that care is taken about the volcanoes in your life?

Now look at these suggestions and plan to alter your current boundaries as you want.

Area	Suggestion
Emotional	Giving time to express emotions when you can.
Relationships	Ensuring that you have boundaries that ensure you protect yourself and self-respect.
Physical	Letting people know what is acceptable in terms of physical space.
Financial	Having a budget and sticking to it.
Time, strength, and energy	Learning about your time, strength and energy and how to use them wisely, e.g. taking breaks. Giving yourself moments to replenish your energy levels.
Cognitive capacities	Using effective strategies for thinking, decision making, remembering and paying attention.
Problem solving	Using effective and collaborative problem-solving approaches that are grounded. Where there is a good balance between the use of logic and emotion. Being realistic about the problem.
Self-care	Ensuring that you are looking after yourself healthily, being mindful of the calm breaths and triggers for the volcanoes.

Area	Boundary
Emotional	
Relationships	
Physical	
Financial	

Time, strength, and energy	
Cognitive capacities	
Problem solving	
Self-care	

VALUES, MOTIVATION, AND PURPOSE

These are the components that can be our guide, our North Star, if we let them. Having reflected on your own, what would you like to change? How will you ensure you use them in your daily life? How will you replenish your motivation?

SELF-CARE

Our lives are usually so busy that we forget to look after ourselves, especially when we are tired, flummoxed or in a time when our past and negatives overwhelm us. So it is vital that we look at our plans for self-care, both for ordinary times and for when we become flummoxed or stressed. Think about how you look after yourself in the areas outlined below and then plan to make the changes.

Area	Day to day	When flummoxed and stressed
Food and drink (A good balance of healthy food (proteins, etc.) and liquids to stay hydrated)		
Activity, e.g. exercise (A reasonable amount of exercise per week, considering health issues)		
Sleep (ensuring a good amount of sleep)		
Breathing (practising regular slow and deep breathing)		
Emotional support (having good assistance)(being able to healthily manage emotions)		

VOLCANOES AND CALM BREATHS

Healing is a continuous journey where we need to acknowledge the myriad volcanoes in our lives and then find a place for them. Ignoring or denying them never works. They just bide their time and re-appear, usually at a very awkward moment.

Here are some exercises to use and keep repeating. Repetition helps.

First, think about what is positive in your life, including the calm breaths and then find ways of increasing their use in your daily life.

Second, please use one or more of these exercises repeatedly so that you can locate the volcanoes and their triggers. Knowing this will lessen their effect and impact.

Find a quiet time and place when you can relax. Practise some breathing. Think about your positives and energies.

Then, itemise your volcanoes in order of impact. Choose one that you want to focus on. If you can't remember it, think about the associated sensations, emotions and behaviours.

Where does the volcano affect you? Body, mind, emotions? How is it triggered? What are your reactions?

Now imagine that you have a powerful vacuum. Switch it on and let it "vacuum" up all parts of the volcano.

Once that is 'finished", take a moment to sense the void that is left. How does it feel? Do you want to keep the void or fill it with something positive? Imagine either keeping it or filling it. Switch off the vacuum. How do you feel?

Imagine you are sitting on a bench in a private garden. You could have a good and trusted friend with you. In front of you is your timeline of your history and two 'baskets'- one for things to destroy and the second for things to keep.

Breathe and keep relaxed. Look at your timeline and 'select' the things you want to keep and place them in the basket for keeping. Then 'identify' the things that you want to destroy and put them in the second basket. Imagine that you are pouring something onto the second basket that will destroy it and the contents. How do you feel?

Now look at the first basket and think about how those issues and memories will help you. Store these somewhere safe so you can return to them when needed.

Again, you can repeat this exercise as much as you want.

Sometimes volcanoes are based on a single memory. If this is the case, then it is likely that the memory has gained extra significance by its emotional loading. You can reduce this to an ordinary memory by safely looking at what happened. It is important not to relive what occurred. But just think about what the learning is for you. How would you act differently? Do you need to forgive yourself or anyone else? What do you need to let go of?

MY PLAN

Please create your plan for the following areas. How will you know you have grown? Who could help and support you? What will you do to make sure that you are reality oriented and realistic?

My future self
Changing
Boundaries
Values, motivation, and purpose
Self-care
Volcanoes and calm breaths

Here is a template you could use.

I am _____

I will be _____

I facilitate my change by _____

My boundaries will be _____

My values, motivation and purpose are _____

I will look after myself by _____

I will manage my volcanoes by _____

I will enhance my calm breaths by _____

People who will help me are _____

Time frame _____

We wish you all the best. Thank you.

Please contact us if you have questions.
info@healthyleadership.world.

References are available on our website
www.healthyleadership.world

Lightning Source UK Ltd.
Milton Keynes UK
UKHW020855080223
416625UK00015B/224